I0486900

Philosophical Considerations Around the Death Penalty

Filippo Fracas

Copyright © 2024 Filippo Fracas
All rights reserved.
ISBN: 978-1-4457-2779-0
Imprint: Lulu.com

Translated by Suzanne Barbeau and Linda Barbeau-Tufts.

CONTENTS

INTRODUCTION

At a young age, a child is taught not to harm others, behave well, and respect others. The child is taught that violence is not the solution for any reason. Respecting the boundaries of a person is critical to a child's upbringing. Despite this known fact, it has caused contradictions to the implementation of respect for a child's viewpoint regarding aggressive behavior. On the one hand, the child is forbidden from using aggression in his daily actions to achieve his goals and justify his conduct.

A clear violation of the principle of non-contraction, which would have immediately startled Aristotle. The parallel between this domestic situation and that of the relationship between the State and the individual is obvious: the State prohibits killing but it itself is the first to do so!

Obviously, the question is not that simple or, at least, it needs deeper analysis of all the variables that compose it. It is useful to clarify what is meant by the term "punishment." The common definition, as stated in a dictionary, is that of "physical or moral damage sanctioned by law as a specific consequence of the crime and imposed by judicial authority through trial." Already in this way, some characteristic features are evident: it is sanctioned by the law, and it is the normative effect (precisely sanctioned by the law) of the crime causes.

Therefore, according to this definition, there is no punishment without the law. Which, therefore, determines it, and above all valorizes it. As such, that is, as physical or moral damage or violence, making it permitted and lawful. This series of attributes that cover the concept of punishment are fundamental because they qualify it as such, elevating it to a higher level than simple punishment and violence. The latter is forbidden, condemned, and almost completely transformed into a crime in the most advanced societies, and constantly controlled by states to prevent it from reaching too high a level, which would be harmful for the state itself. Because precisely the latter allows a redefinition and requalification of violence in punishment, so that the latter assumes the guarantee for the survival of the state itself. Indeed, we could say that it is precisely its condition of existence: It requires a precise and defined social order, structured according to rules, codified in laws, and which are made inviolable thanks to the introduction of punishment because of their violation. A second important consideration regarding the concept of punishment is its new moral identify. It loses the negative connotation that is commonly associated with violence and takes on a positive one, as it is linked to justice, goodness, and fairness.

By stating this, however, a premise is implied: that of the coincidence between the idea of good and justice that citizens possess and that it too, may be reflected in the laws of the state. These two positions do not always coincide. The democratic state should represent the popular position of its citizens. It is possible but not unusual, that discrepancies occur between the democratic state and the political opinions of its citizens. Derrida, himself, has illustrated this in the Seminars about the death penalty. He presented the results of two referendums on the abolition of the death penalty which occurred in France and the Unted States. It is noted that there is much dissent between keeping the death penalty or disposing of it altogether. In one decision about abolishing the death penalty, the Constitutional Court decided to maintain it, and in the latter, the opposite happened.

The situation created breaks that structural concatenation between citizens and the state typical of every democracy. At least this happened temporarily, and then the congruence between the two positions was restored.

FIRST PART

The nature of the punishment.

Punishment can take various forms: corporal, psychological, custodial, and pecuniary and finally, the death penalty.

In almost all current societies, prison sentences and financial penalties are the most widespread, which are both applied respectively, for major and minor crimes.

Today, the punishment has taken on a varied and different value depending on the nation. For countries which have a corrective purpose and where the criminal possesses, as a citizen and/or human being, certain inviolable rights, for which the punishment consists in a violation temporary or definitive release from prison (detention), or a confiscation of one or more assets of a patrimonial nature (financial penalty), to those nations in which the use of physical or psychological punishments is lawful and finally, to countries in which the two concepts are intertwined.

In the latter, perhaps the most striking example is that of the United States, which, despite belonging to the group of democratic countries and therefore, defining itself as the guarantor of human rights, allows the death penalty in its own state (in this regard, the discussion regarding the Vill article of the American Constitution).

This might seem like a contradiction, but it would be simplified.

In fact, such a serious punishment, such as capital punishment, is considered lawful because it guarantees precisely those fundamental human rights that every democratic country has incorporated into its constitution (including the USA itself).

Furthermore, the considerations just expressed allow us to address another fundamental problem, that of the justification of punishment.

The latter is at the center of the "Theory of Punishment," that is, the theory that attempts to answer the question "why punish?".

The justification of punishment has its roots in the broader Theory of Justice.

Therefore, in the large and complex theoretical system that

deals with which behaviors are considered lawful and which are not, consequently, which ones to punish, how to do it, how to decide the correct punishment and who has the right to punish.

The underlying dichotomy is that between being and having to be, between *sollen* and *sein*: the crucial point is determining what is right and what is not but above all whether being right is so because it is moral or because the law decides it, and it is still necessary to divide between an association between law and nature and law as a single construction.

We thus distinguish natural law, for which the rights of man (when we speak of "man," according to some, could extend the validity of natural law, but also to other living beings, such as animals) are dictated by nature.

They are the property of man by nature, and legal positivism where, on the contrary, the law is pure separated from any form of infiltration of morality, or other, in thus coinciding with a human product.

The question of punishment and its justification must be placed in a specific context, which depends on its implications and its equally specific result.

In fact, if morality were used as a criterion, one would attempt to determine a punishment morally adequate to the committed crime but in no case lower than a certain level of morality, otherwise the field of immorality would be invaded and as the English say, finally, we must analyze what we mean by fact.

If, however, we wanted to trace the justification of punishment back to certain specific laws of the judicial system, we would only be positioning the problem, since the above-mentioned system must also be justified.

CHAPTER 2

Comparison of two Conceptions of Law

Legal positivism considers that the only valid law is natural law. It claims that there exists an objective and universal right valid for all men, as such, by nature and independently of any agreement or acceptance on their part.

There is obviously a close relationship between morality and law, that is, man has certain fundamental rights by nature and the said rights are also morally right.

Consequently, any form of (positive) human right, product of the culture of human society, can only tend to reflect natural law, without ever reaching it and will be equitable to the extent that it succeeds in achieving it.

Several important declarations were written according to the principles of natural law, such as, *the United States of America Declaration of Independence* signed on July 4, 1776 as a manifesto illustrating the reasons why the thirteen colonies claimed their independence from England: the *Declaration of Rights of Man and of the Citizen* (*Déclaration des Droits de* *l'Homme et du Citoyen)*written in 1789 presented as the maximum expression of the principles of the French Revolution, which owes much to illuminism; *The Universal Declaration of Human rights* of 1948 was promoted by the United Nations.

The order in which these statements were expressed is not random but reflects a relationship of concatenation between them: the first influenced the second which, in turn, influenced the third, and all three were the basis of numerous constitutions of different contemporary democratic states. This last aspect is very important because it appears as a bridge between natural law and legal positivism: natural rights are the basis of the declarations that we have just listed, which however have influenced various constitutions, which in turn are the foundations of all legal systems.

There are still several points to address if we come back to the conception of natural law. Mainly the conception of "Nature", which, as Bobbio says, is one of the haziest concepts in the history of philosophy: even in works on the subject (Hobbes, Rousseau, Thomas Aquinas), there is no agreement on the question whether the state of nature is peaceful or not, whether the inborn instinct is favorable to society or whether man in this state is strong or weak.

Secondly, the values on which natural law is based constitute an unjustified starting point. In fact, if they were definitive, the problem of knowing how man was able to determine them would arise as well as the reason why they are precisely so; to anyone who answers these questions that the guarantor of their correctness is human rationality, one might wonder what we mean by that and what is the link between rationality and nature.

If rationality were accepted as a means to arrive at truth, it would not be possible to demonstrate the existence of a rationality of nature. Moreover, in order to find an order and a justification for a thesis in Nature, we fall into error due to what we call the "*naturalistic fallacy*" which, as Hume and Moore say, tends to assimilate the descriptive to the prescriptive, the *being* to the *ought to be*.

The second orientation of the philosophy of law that we wish to address is that of legal positivism. Its main thesis is that law coincides with positive law, that is, with what I believe and not what it should be, with the facts. It is always inserted in a specific historical context and is such because it is dictated by a sovereign authority (willingness) and codified in laws.

Legal positivism therefore presents itself as the opposite of natural law: it rejects any association between law and nature or between law and morality.

Law is not an expression of the natural order, there are no absolute and a priori values to any law formulation or its acceptance by all those subject to it.

Instead, we try to place the acceptance of law as the first condition of its existence and establish a legal system that has no external support, such as morality or nature, but which maintains internal consistency. For supporters of equal positivism, the law is itself a guarantee, in the sense that it respects its own completeness and internal coherence.

Legal positivism is based on two different attitude of law, one ideological-political and the other scientific: for the first, the law, as a manifestation of the will of the sovereign (identified with that of the legislator), manifests itself in laws and coercion as social control and, for the second, it must have a specific and well-defined structure, with scientific bases and therefore highlights the objectivity of the law, canceling any trace of arbitrary.

Various criticisms have been addressed to legal positivism, among which the most important are hiding an inevitable acceptance of the law as it is and therefore, since the presence of an absolute absence of ideology is impossible, implicitly supporting the ideology contained in existing law and, ultimately, consistent support and acceptance from those in power. Unlike natural law, however, legal positivism is more complex, more varied and contains different, more internal currents, such as the normativism of Hans Kelsen, who faced many of the criticisms leveled at the first conception of legal positivism.

CHAPTER 3

The Law between the State and the Individual

For a complete discussion of law, one must address the relationship connection that exists between the state and the individual, the way in which the law itself structures this relationship, and the definition of justice that follows from it.

Depending on how the concepts of state and individual are intertwined there are two different states and anti-statism.

For the first position, supported especially by legal positivists, state law is the only possible one, therefore law is truly such, in its highest development, only in the modern and contemporary State: in fact, this conception of law was very widespread in the nineteenth century.

However, it does not explain forms of law that cannot be linked to a single and defined state sovereignty, such as international law.

Nevertheless, according to anti-statists, law is not a product of the State or linked to it.

Strong support for this position comes from legal pluralism, according to which the presence of several different forms of state within the same territory (in addition to that recognized as a state) is possible.

Alongside these two theses, there is a third of a different nature from the previous ones: the legalization of the State. The latter would no longer be central in the formulation of the law but would, on the contrary, also find its basis in the law itself.

In fact, Kelsey's legal positivism goes so far as to argue that law is a system of rules that regulate the use of force, which may or may not have a state origin.

Thus, with the process of jurisdiction we come to argue that the State is nothing other than a pure legal product and that it has such a structure due to its identity as a legal mechanism (which produces laws and enforces them while punishing transgressors), depriving any other discipline (political, moral, religious) of the possibility of intervening in the very conception of the State.

A particular form of relationship between law and the state is the so-called "*rule of law*".

The law becomes the skeleton of the State, it constitutes it and represents its guarantee.

In fact, it is the same law that governs not only the actions of individuals but also those of the State since all power and all use of force must be controlled in accordance with the law.

The rule of law is therefore subject to the so-called principle of legality, which controls and limits the power of the State towards the individual, thus protecting their freedom, and allowing them a relationship of equality in law towards the State itself.

This contrasts sharply with the absolute state, where the power of the latter is unconditional and unlimited.

Considering laws as a measure of guaranteeing the justice of a State is based on the consideration that they are impartial, neutral, stable, and safe, and general.

This is unlike the mutability and subjectivity of human passions. This would provoke personal judgement and would result from the mood of the moment, also capable of transforming justice into revenge.

Even if the idea of being right has a strong utopian connotation, it is also possible to take forms before all to avoid the appearance of a tyranny, noting that the limit of possibility can be found in the inviolability of the natural rights of an individual (*the natural Law of the philosophy of*

Enlightenment), equally justifying a rebellion in cases of breaking of the social pact which is intact and which establishes obedience to a sovereign (right of resistance). And in forming of a constitution here represents the basis of the legal system, the State of Law has become constitutional.

These two law positions are linked to a long historical past, since (as can be seen) the formation of a constitutional State is precisely a consequence of proclaiming natural rights fundamental (even if they do not necessarily coincide).

The fundamental characteristic of the constitutional state is the presence of a Constitutional Charter (compliance with which, in contemporary times, is controlled by the Constitutional Court, outlined by Hans Kelsen) which establishes and limits the powers of a State towards the individual recalling an untouchable sphere of freedom (thoughts, words, opinions) but also repairing the rights of citizens themselves.

Furthermore, The State of law guarantees all rights linked to the human rights so that the same guarantees are the legitimation and justification of the right.

Following this directive, in order to establish a linear relationship between the group of individuals with their moral ideas and the state, who does not absolutely hold the moral objective truth must respect the truth of the individual subjects composing the State: it is clear that the theory of re-education would not be authorized.

Secondly, I would also like to consider the great influence of Montesquieu's "*The Spirit of the Laws*" ("*L'Esprit des Lois*" - 1743), which exposes the principle of the separation and independence of powers, so that each part can be a guarantee and a limit for the others.

Another consideration concerns the difference between the rule of law and democracy: The former bases itself and the power that comes with it on the law.

Consequently, it cannot allow its institutions to depend on any power, including the power of the people, which is expressed after a democratic election.

Finally, although the Rule of Law is based on laws, their nature must be better specified: in the first place, they must be objective, certain, precise, of firm and unquestionable clarity, to ensure that their interest is not subjective or free, even creative; in the second place, however, it is necessary to avoid subjecting them to excessive formalism that would lead them to change from means to ends.

This theory, called Ethical Formalism, leads to an

extremism of the principle of legality and simplifies compliance with the law, because it imposes blind and absolute obedience to the laws, widening the gap between morality and law.

To conclude this paragraph, we must briefly refer to the concept of justice: legal equality must be reserved for different citizens belonging to the same state.

If we have emphasized the guarantee of laws as a means of impersonal and objective application of the law, especially as regards the rule of law and its current development towards a constitutional state, a simple comparison with everyday reality will suffice to show how the gap between this ideal and the concrete realization is becoming ever wider. Indeed, it could be clearly said that the Law is personal, in the sense that it takes on different forms depending on whom it is intended to affect.

Indeed, sentences are often cultural products rather than the rigorous outcome of legal proceedings.

In the United States, for example, the number of death sentences handed down to African Americans is statistically higher than to whites.

Racism is much more influential than any law, and this is compounded by having to interpret.

Although the laws are defined, it is very difficult for any lawyer, even the most experienced, to determine their correct application. Therefore, there is a wide margin of discretion.

In fact, it is not even possible to speak of justice, and any application of it through an act of interpretation is purely arbitrary and creative, according to the legal philosopher Hans Kelsen.

The law, like any other theoretical system, is a human product and, like any other (science first and foremost), it is not immune to error, and, above all, it will never reach the degree of absoluteness and objectivity that is expected of it.

Today, in most of the existing states, the form of government is democratic, but it bases its law on a single basis, the constitutional statute, from which positive law is formed, starting from natural law.

We try to make the law moral. Even if we are not sure what it is.

CHAPTER 4

Theories on Punishment

Let us return to the theory of punishment, and to the most important theories of punishment, namely the theory of retribution and the theory of prevention.

Retributive theories hold that punishment is an end, resulting from the crime committed.

Therefore, punishment is not a means to an end, such as the criminal's awareness of the crime committed and subsequent re-education, but an end: the famous law of retribution, present in the Babylonian King Hammurabi's Code, is supported, causing evil (crime) must suffer equally evil (punishment).

The retributive theory consists of three variants: The moral version, which states that the crime is a voluntary violation of the ethical order by a subject and considers punishment as its restoration; the legal version, which sees the crime as a rebellion of the individual will against the law and therefore against the legal system (which is an expression of the dominant power, according to legal positivism) and therefore punishment is a reaffirmation of it; The third and last is the denunciatory version, which sees punishment as expressing (in the form of denunciation) the community's anger against the moral evil of crime, with the consequent strengthening of social unity.

According to retributivism, the application (and thus the justification) of punishment is subject to various moral limits: only those who have committed a direct transgression and whose guilt is clear, fully conscious, and unjustified (except for insanity and pretext) can be punished; furthermore, there must be a proportion between the punishment and the crime (and this is one of the most difficult problems).

We seek to protect individual freedom from the state's punitive power.

Various criticisms have been placed on the retributive theory First, it is not self-justifying, i.e., it does not explain the moral thesis according to which, once an evil (crime) has been committed, another evil (punishment) is necessary to restore the good and, in general, the purpose of punishment. The second theory of punishment is preventive. In contrast to the first one, it is more projective, that is, the punishment is considered as a deterrent for possible future criminal acts: the fear of punishment should discourage the commission of a criminal act. Prevention theory also includes several variations of itself.

The first is the theory of general prevention, which claims that the preventive factor lies in the threat of punishment, thus expressing a solid faith in the criminal law and its potential as a means of controlling and repressing threats such as criminal acts.

The second is the theory of punishment that sees the application of punishment to concrete cases as a useful means of prevention at the more general level: the famous adage "punish one, teach one hundred" applies, that is, the punishment of one individual, often swift and disproportionate to the crime committed, becomes the means used to achieve social objectives.

The third is the theory of special prevention, which places punishment on a more individual and personal level, focusing on the criminal as an individual rather than on the crime he has committed. It has two different objectives: to re-educate the offender or to neutralize him from committing new crimes. In this respect, there is a tendency to make punishment as personal as possible (possibly violating principles such as equality or legality).

The re-education of the delinquent involves the presence of specific problems, first that of personal freedom. In fact, the latter is the basis of every democracy and of the concept of man in contemporary society as the owner of his own destiny and his capacity for self-determination.

The re-education of an individual would establish a relationship of force between the State and the individual, in which the former would force the latter to undergo a forced transformation of his or her identity, violating his or her privacy and his or her mentality.

In this way, the individual would no longer be a criminal to be punished, but a sick person to be healed; the relationship established would thus pass from a horizontal to a vertical dimension, of dominance and superiority of the State over the individual criminal, who has now assumed the appearance of a lost child and therefore not to be blamed.

Like retributivism, the theory of prevention is not self-sufficient because it does not specify why prevention works to reduce crime, nor does it specify which actions to prevent and by what means.

CHAPTER 5

SECOND PART

Punishment according to the Enlightenment philosopher Rousseau.

The Age of Enlightenment is a period in the history of mankind (second half of the 18th century) identified by specific characteristics, such as the strong confidence in reason as a means for man to escape "the state of minority that he must ascribe to himself: (as Kant replied in 1784 to the question What is the Enlightenment?), to know reality and improve it, to critically confront prejudices and the dogmatisms of the past, ascribed to religions or authorities. But if these premises suggest a total condemnation of any violation of the individual himself, such as capital punishment, the Geneva philosopher does not agree.

Rousseau is one of the founding fathers of democracy, because he succeeded in establishing a contract, a social contract, which allows for a balance between the State, on the one hand, and the individual, on the other hand, according to which the latter succeeds in establishing a contract as the basis of their life in society, while respecting their freedom as free agents (indeed, "man is born free and everywhere he is in chains"). He therefore encounters all those philosophical and theological theories according to which the origin of society and its resulting institutions is divine or natural.

The individual, according to the provisions of the contract, although he benefits from the protection and security of the State, always remains free within it and in his relation to the law, because he makes it his own equal part and represents its foundation, like all the others: equality, typical of the natural State, is also preserved in the social State.

In fact, each person loses his or her value as a unique individual and accepts the other as a member of a community that he or she has helped to create. In this society, where she must make concessions as in a social contract, she makes the right to be free coincide with the need to be subject to a society (coincidence between citizen and subject).

Rousseau addresses the problem of punishment and its justification in the new context of the social contract in chapter V of the Social Contract (Amsterdam, 1762), entitled *On the Right of Life and Death*. The argument is subtle but coherent.

First, "everyone has the right to risk his own life in order to preserve it" and "the social contract has as its goal the loyalty of the contracting parties", but, in a tone reminiscent of Machiavelli, he maintains that those who want an end also accept the means to achieve it, therefore "those who want to preserve their life with the help of others must also, if necessary, give it for them".

The same reasoning applies to capital punishment, although the parties who agree to be killed are not so free. But to prevent the law from being invaded by criminals and to preserve the State (and the contract), it seems inevitable that "in order not to be the victim of an assassination, one agrees to die in the event that one would become a murderer.

In fact, the culprit would be considered an enemy of the community and therefore eliminated in the event of a breach of contract.

Therefore, the criminal who is guilty of violating the contract deserves death (if necessary). But Rousseau does not stop there, he questions the state itself, because "the frequency of torture is always a sign of weakness or indolence on the part of the government.

As for the granting of grace, this implies that one is above the law and the judge, and this can only be done by the sovereign body, the maximum expression of the covenant, which does it.

But, on the other hand, "in a well-governed state there are few punishments, not because there are many pardons, but because there are few criminals: the multiplicity of crimes ensures impunity when the state is in decline.

Finally, it is very interesting to note (in the context of the debate on the justification of punishment, as already mentioned) the criticism of the theory by the Geneva philosopher as an example: "We have no right to put to death, for example, that which cannot be preserved without .anger".

In summary, we can affirm that Rousseau does not justify the death penalty (or punishment in general) in principle, but only to the extent that it is contextualized in the social contract, as an instrument (however extreme) of its preservation, while fully demonstrating the power that the contract assumes over its contractors.

CHAPTER 6

Philosophical support for Retributive Theory: the main lines of Hegel's philosophy of law

G.W.G. Hegel is considered the greatest exponent of the retributive theory used to justify capital punishment (and punishment in general).

In order to understand his position, it is of course necessary to frame it in the work which deals with these questions, namely *Elements of the Philosophy of Right* (the work thanks to which the term "philosophy of right" was introduced).

This procedure does not violate the usual tripartite dynamic of thesis (law), antithesis (violation of the law by the crime) and synthesis (affirmation of the law itself); the main thesis is that punishment is necessary to cancel the denial of the right, a consequence of the crime, by negating the negation, restoring the violated right and thus guaranteeing the full realization of the offender's freedom (understood as the freedom to obey the will of the law, which is an expression of the will of the Absolute Spirit).

Hegel addresses these topics in the first part, which deals with Abstract Law (which, together with Morality and Ethics, represents the three stages of the Hegelian dialectic within the Objective Spirit).

In the third part, Part C, entitled _Coercion and Crime_, he further divides it into two parts: _Coercion_ and _Crime and Punishment_.

The point we want to make will be mainly about these parts. We will try to trace a path that leads from the first part to the second.

Coercion explains the coercive nature of abstract law in response to the coercion experienced through crime: "Abstract law is coercive law. The violation of this law is, in fact, the violence exercised against the existence of my freedom in an external thing. The preservation of this existence against violence is therefore itself an external action and a violence that suppresses this first violence.

With these words, Hegel summarizes well the dialectical process that will find its maximum expression in the following part: coercion as punishment is the consequence of coercion as crime.

The discussion that follows starts from the externalization of the will in the property, "in the property, my will places itself in an external thing: and as a consequence of the aforementioned process, the presence of coercion and its relation to the will: "*From this point of view, my will can, on the one hand, generally be subjected to violence, while, on the other hand, a sacrifice or an action can be imposed with violence as a condition of a certain possession or positivity: in the latter case, a constraint is exerted on my will*".

In this passage, the distinction between violence and coercion is emphasized, since the latter, unlike the former, has a positive value.

But as is often the case in Hegelian philosophy, the question is not so simple. If, on the one hand, coercion is considered illegitimate because it destroys the will, on the other hand, it becomes necessary when it presents itself as a "*second coercion*". "*The fact that coercion, in its own concept, is self-destructive, has its reality when exposed in this form: coercion is removed by coercion. Coercion is therefore not only legal in a certain conditioned sense, but also necessary as a second coercion, which constitutes the removal of a first coercion.*"

Coercion therefore has a double value, but this does not mean that it is arbitrary; in fact, just as each element of the Hegelian system has its own precise place, the same is true of the two values assumed by coercion: it destroys the will, but precisely because of this capacity it succeeds in its task of destroying the destroyer, leading to the elimination of itself through itself.

We have Hegel's subtle justification of punishment, the basis of criminal law, which he will examine in the second part, Crime and Punishment, in this process, which takes place in different phases of the usual dialectical process.

But first, in order to have a complete conceptual framework, it is useful to briefly recall the beginning of this third section, The Illegal Act, where the philosopher illustrates the necessity of The Illegal Act so that we can move from law in itself as an entity in relation to real and effective law: "*This phenomenon of the law - this appearance in which the law itself coincides immediately, that is to say, accidentally, with its essential existence, with the particular will - is transformed in the illicit into an appearance, yes, the illicit is transformed in the contrast between the right in itself and a particular will, in which it becomes a particular right*".

Now the truth of this appearance consists in this: the appearance itself is something empty, and the law, through the negation of its negation, re-establishes itself.

The Hegelian conception of law is therefore totally different and incommensurable with the theories of law presented so far, in the sense that law neither arises nor results from the nature of individuals nor from their agreement, but is rather incomplete as long as its essence, which is universal, remains linked to an accidental harmony with the particular will, that linked to individuals, thus generating a "particular law" that can reveal itself precisely thanks to the illicit act (through the negation of the negation).

After this general survey of the law, to find a connection between it and coercion, we now want to return specifically to the (already almost sketched) connection between crime and punishment.

In the above-mentioned second part (Crime and Punishment), Hegel opens the discussion as follows: "*The first coercion which, as the exercise of violence by a free being, is injurious to the existence of freedom in its concrete sense* [...] *is a crime. Crime, in its fullest sense, is a judgment that is negatively infinite. By this judgment not only the particular is denied* [...] *but at the same time also the universal*".

With these words, he presents the crime as a negation and then specifies the different degrees of seriousness. This negation, a violation of the law, results in a subsequent restoration of the crime This occurs through punishment. The latter, however, appears as a right of the criminal, as a rational being, and is based on retributive justice:

"*The suppression of crime is retribution to the extent that (1) it is, according to the concept, an injury to injury, and (2) crime, according to existence, has a specific, qualitative and quantitative extension, so that even the negation of crime, as existence, has the same extension*".

Finally, Hegel stresses that criminal law must not be based on revenge, which only generates new injuries, but on punishment, so that *"justice is freed both from the subjectivity of interest and figure and from the accidental character of Power."*

CONCLUSION

To solve these problems, we started with a simple domestic example that everyone can observe: A child who is punished with violence for disobeying a parent or relative, perhaps because he has behaved violently toward another child.

A scene perhaps banal but certainly full of meaning if you can grasp it.

In fact, we are surrounded by similar logical paradoxes, which hide other intentions, but which want to appear perfectly normal: the death penalty is one of them.

Although there are different philosophical and logical positions that support it, guaranteeing it a solid theoretical basis, and that the validity of a truth must always be contextualized each time in the environment where it is found, its abolition is progressing in many countries and its conceptual base is developing, collapsing under the blows of a mixture of humanism and empiricism of associations like Amnesty International and others.

We tend to invalidate it in the human context, which is the

one in which it was born, by exploiting its uselessness as a preventative measure or as being amoral and free from all rights, today the first defender of life. The death penalty does not relieve the victim's families and abandons that of the condemned or hides unconscious collective or individual violence, especially if there are dictators in power.

But we know, man has always abounded in words, it is the facts that he lacks.

BIBLIOGRAPHY AND WEBSITES

➤ Georg Wilhelm Friedrich Hegel, Lineamenti di filosofia del diritto, Vincenzo Cicero (a cura di), Milano, Rusconi libri, 1996, pagg. 193-215 per le note dalle 10 alle 17;

➤ Jean Jacques Rousseau, Contratto sociale, Diego Giordano (a cura di), Milano, Bompiani, 2012, pagg. 407-411 per le note dalla 2 alla 9;

➤ Jean-Jacques Chevallier, Le grandi opere del pensiero politico, Bologna, il Mulino (Le vie della civiltà), 1998;

➤ Guido Baldi, Silvia Giusso, Mario Razetti, Giuseppe Zaccaria, La letteratura Vol. 3 dal Barocco all'Illuminismo, Milano, Paravia, 2007;

➤ Nicola Zingarelli (a cura di), Il Nuovo Zingarelli, Vocabolario della lingua italiana, Bologna, Zanichelli, 1983 per la nota 1;

➤ http://www.fondazionealegrilletti.com/documenti/grillore.pdf;

➤ http://www.wikipedia.org.

Filippo Fracas graduated in philosophy from the University of Milan; he is the author of a philosophical novel entitled "*I sogni di Joan*", published in 2015 by GDS Edizioni, and of "*Critiche epistemologiche alla psicoanalisi (le tesi di Wittgenstein e Popper)* by Biblioteca Filosofica PE, published in 2020, as well as several articles from Academia.edu. including the one published and translated in this essay.

www.ingramcontent.com/pod-product-compliance
Lightning Source LLC
Chambersburg PA
CBHW051248170526
45165CB00004B/1620